Lifecycles

# Egg to Chicken

## Camilla de la Bédoyère

QED Publishing

Copyright © QED Publishing 2009

First published in the UK in 2009 by
QED Publishing
A Quarto Group company
226 City Road
London EC1V 2TT

www.qed-publishing.co.uk

A catalogue record for this book is available
from the British Library.

ISBN 978 1 84835 170 7

Printed and bound in China

**Author** Camilla de la Bédoyère
**Editor** Angela Royston
**Designer and Picture Researcher** Melissa Alaverdy

**Publisher** Steve Evans
**Creative Director** Zeta Davies
**Managing Editor** Amanda Askew

Words in **bold** are explained in the glossary on page 22.

**Picture credits**
(t=top, b=bottom, l=left, r=right, c=centre, fc=front cover)
**Corbis** 1t Holger Winkler/AB/zefa, 1b Craig Holmes/Loop Images, 5t Martin Harvey, 6–7 Craig Holmes/Loop Images, 11b Holger Winkler/AB/zefa
**Getty Images** 10–11 Georgette Douwma, 11t Bob Elsdale, 12 Dorling Kindersley, 15b Tara Moore, 17t Jane Burton, 17b GK Hart/ Vikki Hart, 18 Klaus Nigge
**Photolibrary Group** 9t John Cancalosi, 13 Harald Lange, 14 Andre Maslennikov, 20–21 Harald Lange
**Shutterstock** 2t iofoto, 4b Dee Hunter, 4–5 Valio, 5b JanJar, 6b JanJar, 6t Gelpi, 8 Craig Hanson, 8 Craig Hanson, 9b Babusi Octavian Florentin, 15t AGphotographer, 16b Saied Shahin Kiya, 16c Saied Shahin Kiya, 16t Saied Shahin Kiya, 19 Babusi Octavian Florentin, 20l Jozsef Szasz-Fabian, 22–23 Vasyl Helevachuk, 24 Saied Shahin Kiya

# Contents

# What is a chicken?

A chicken is a type of bird. All birds have feathers and wings, and all birds lay eggs.

Feathers help birds to fly, and to stay warm and dry. Flying takes a lot of energy, so birds need to eat often.

⇩Birds have mouths called beaks or bills, but no teeth.

⇧ Gulls spread their wings and feathery tails when they fly.

Not all birds can fly. Ostriches have wings, but cannot fly. Ostriches are the world's largest birds. Some are more than 2 metres tall.

Ostrich egg

⇧ Ostrich feathers are long, soft and fluffy.

⇨One ostrich egg weighs the same as 24 hen eggs.

Hen egg

# The story of a chicken

There are more chickens in the world than any other type of bird.

A hen is a female chicken. A male chicken is called a rooster or a cockerel. A chick is a baby chicken.

Chicks begin their lives as eggs. The story of how an egg grows into an adult chicken is called a **life cycle**.

⇨ A chicken goes through three stages in its life cycle.

Chick

2

1

Egg

3

Adult chicken

# Making a nest

Hens start laying eggs when they are around six months old. First, they need a **nest** to lay the eggs in.

Most birds build their nests in trees. They may use twigs, grass or moss.

⇦ Ospreys build huge nests of twigs in trees and on rooftops.

⇨ The smallest nests are built by hummingbirds.

Hens build their nests on the ground. They find somewhere dry and quiet, and use straw or grass to make the nest.

⇨ Hens build their nests in barns or hen houses, where they are warm and safe.

# The eggs are laid

A hen usually lays one egg a day. The eggs will only grow into chicks if the hen has already **mated** with a rooster.

When a rooster wants to mate, he crows loudly. As they mate, the rooster **fertilizes** the hen's eggs.

⇦ A rooster also crows to tell other males to stay away.

⇨Roosters are bigger than hens and they have longer tail feathers.

◊The hen starts to lay her eggs a day after mating.

Only fertilized eggs can grow into chicks. A group of eggs is called a clutch.

# Brooding

When the hen ... a clutch of eggs
in the nest ... the hen ...
to keep ... This ...
called brooding ...
is an impor...

The hen ...
hen clutch ...
chicks grow ...
eggs ... cold, the
chicks stop growing.

⇨ A brooding hen
spreads her feathers
over the eggs.

The hen and the rooster look after their eggs.
They want the hen and rooster eggs.

The hen turns the eggs from time to time. The hen uses her own body to keep them warm all over the eggs.

13

# Inside the egg

All bird eggs are protected by a hard **shell**. Inside each fertilized egg, a tiny chick is growing.

Yolk

Chick

Albumen

Shell

Inside the egg, the chick gets food from the yellow **yolk** and **albumen**. The albumen is the clear liquid that we call the white of the egg. It protects the chick and keeps it warm.

⇐ Chicks need air to breathe. The larger end of the egg holds an air space.

14

Hens lay eggs even when they have not mated. The eggs we eat have not been fertilized. They don't have chicks inside them.

⇧ Most chicken egg shells are brown, white or cream.

⇨ Chicken eggs are easy to cook, and good to eat!

# The eggs hatch

After growing for about three weeks, the young chicks are ready to break out of their eggs. This is called **hatching**.

Each chick has a sharp point on their top beak, called an egg-tooth.

3

2

1

⇧ It uses its body to push the shell apart.

⇦ It chips a hole all round the shell.

⇦ The chick uses its egg-tooth to crack a hole in the shell.

⇦ Then it climbs out of the shell.

The newly hatched chick cheeps loudly. It is tired and its feathers are wet. Once the feathers have dried, they become fluffy.

⇨ Soon all the chicks have hatched out!

4

5

# Life as a chick

The hen looks after her newly hatched chicks. She keeps them warm under her wings.

When they are just two weeks old, the chicks can leave the barn or hen house and explore outside.

⇦ Newly hatched chicks stay close to their mother.

Chicks and chickens like to scratch around in the dirt, looking for tasty worms or bugs to eat.

⇨Chickens do not have teeth, so they cannot chew their food. They swallow it whole instead.

# Growing and changing

The chicks grow into adults in just a few months. Glossy feathers grow in place of the soft, fluffy feathers.

The chicks grow red, fleshy **combs** on top of their heads. The combs help to keep them cool.

⇧ A hen that is less than one year old is called a pullet.

Soon the young hens will start to lay eggs. When a hen mates, a new life cycle begins.

⇩Roosters have colourful feathers and grow larger combs than hens.

Comb

# Glossary

**Albumen**
The white of an egg.

**Brooding**
When a hen sits on her eggs to keep them warm.

**Comb**
The soft, red skin on top of a chicken's head.

**Fertilize**
When a special cell from a male joins with a female's egg to form a new living thing.

**Hatching**
When a chick breaks out of its egg.

**Life cycle**
The story of how an animal changes from birth to death, and how it produces young.

**Mated**
When a male and a female have come together to produce young.

**Nest**
A safe place that birds make where they can lay their eggs.

**Shell**
The hard outside of an egg. It protects the chick inside.

**Yolk**
The yellow part of an egg. The yolk is food for the chick inside the egg.

22

# Index

# Notes for parents and teachers

- Look through the book and talk about the pictures. Read the captions and ask questions about other things in the photographs that have not been mentioned in the text.

- Find out more about birds by watching them in the wild. Help children to use a guidebook to identify different birds. Remind them that nests and eggs should never be approached or disturbed.

- Science at home. Carry out some simple experiments with a hen's egg. Try rolling it on a smooth surface and watch how it moves. See what happens when you float an egg in water (the freshest eggs sink). Open the egg and identify the different parts. Hard boil an egg and talk about the way heat has changed its contents.

- Be prepared for questions about human life cycles. There are plenty of books available for this age group that can help you give age-appropriate explanations.

- Talking about a child's family helps them to link life processes to their own experience. Drawing simple family trees, looking at photos and talking to grandparents are fun ways to engage young children.